FROG SPOTTING

First published in 2009 by
The Dedalus Press
13 Moyclare Road
Baldoyle
Dublin 13
Ireland

www.dedaluspress.com

ISBN 978 1 906614 06 5

Dedalus Press titles are represented in North America
by Syracuse University Press, Inc., 621 Skytop Road,
Suite 110, Syracuse, New York 13244, and in the UK by
Central Books, 99 Wallis Road, London E9 5LN

Cover image © Alexander Copeland/iStockPhoto.com

Dedalus Press receives financial assistance from
The Arts Council / An Chomhairle Ealaíon

FROG SPOTTING

Peggy O'Brien

DEDALUS PRESS
DUBLIN, IRELAND

ACKNOWLEDGEMENTS

Thanks to the editors of the following magazines where these poems (sometimes in slightly different form) originally appeared: "Floating" in *The Irish Times;* "Frog Spotting" in *The South-West Review;* "Mourning Dove" in *The Yale Review;* "Lent" and "Malamute" in *The Bend;* "Painting Blind" in *Poetry Ireland Review;* and "American Shad" in *Watershed.*

for Doodle

Contents

47 Sandford Road

for Mary Ellen Fox and Anne Kelly

I came back to the insanity of roses
unfolding at the sun's sole behest
in a space designed to reflect reason.

Everything was in proportion. A calm
façade. Minimal embellishment. Color
serene and fresh, lemon, celadon.

An agitated guest, I was the ghost
who, when the living were out
and about, had the run of the place.

Random as dust motes, I would settle
on this and that, a painting in a reassuring
frame, silk too fine to touch,

photographs of strong-boned boys
growing up and up without a hitch,
handsome men mounting the staircase.

That house, a class set apart for salvation,
sat back from the road, insulated
from its roar by absorbent trees and grass.

And I was free to choose my window
by my mood. The world was not
about to change, just my view of it.

Now, all the houses on that fortunate
terrace like lounge chairs in the sun
relax at the back into long gardens.

The oblong frame I looked through shaped
the sense of what I saw, each pane
the sovereign facet of a crystal.

More than ever I hovered between
stories on that return, looking out
and over into Helen Dillon's garden.

I studied that gardener's studiously
artless art, how she could tempt
wild roses to trust a trellis,

make radically opposed flowers,
the easy-going daisy and tetchy
iris, just got on with the plan,

a place for every kind of display,
the needy vine, wildly clashing
colors revealing more of each other.

I had the thought that I could float
through glass without breaking it, adored
the sun so much I was the light.

The house returned me to the sanity
of building walls to last, block
upon block until the job is done.

Rainbow Over Dublin Bay

Temporary, another flat in this Old Norse city
Where winter is a past I need to keep revisiting.

Hard with all this murk to see the sunlit
Present, noon, love at a window calling

"Here, come here, from Howth to the mouth of the Liffey,
The view we paid the steep, outrageous rent for."

Sure enough, the fallen angels in black wetsuits
Who congregate below and know how to use the wind

To fly off and cut with their fins chevron tacks
Across the bay, mere sketches of the master plan,

Gathered together and went back up to get it
Right this time, a wide unbroken arc.

Well, not quite. At its zenith it is incomplete,
As though that band got homesick for this earth,

The usual unfinished or abridged story, the ellipsis
Of deep sleep, the potential of a fontanel,

The great torc of Dublin Bay, both exit
And entry. This miracle, however made in Heaven,

Needs like electricity grounding in two points
Of contact. Take a grown man and woman. Bend them

Through the prism of a marriage. You will get
With the exact mixture of sun and rain the entire

Spectrum: red, orange, yellow, green, blue, violet;
Rage, laughter, sorrow, silence, talk and touch,

The arched back of clarity lifting us up
And over that almost always clouded city.

Tea Cozy from Kashmir

i.m. Agha Shahid Ali

January. It's been a year.
You must be almost cosy
Under your cold comforter.

That's, of course, just silly
Poetry. Your soul shivers
Without the fire of your soul.

And that's nothing more
Than the leftover scraps of nursery
Fare from catechism class.

I don't know what or where
You are. I do know the out-
Landish person you were

Comes back on the dot of four
Each day, since I observe
The secular rite of tea.

Bring the water to a rolling
Boil, scald the pot, add
The leaves and hot water,

Leave them steep under
Their soft cover like an egg
In ash for a spell, then pour.

Observing the decorum of the table
We never forked over man-sized
Portions of love and terror.

We engaged in bite-sized small talk,
Cucumber sandwich chat,
Fat sausage rolls of gossip.

We weren't precisely friends.
I was one of scores
Who adored your divine, little ways,

How you cast your bread upon
The waters, always throwing
Parties for no earthly reason

Other than so-and-so, what's-
Her-name, was passing through.
You'd go out to shop for food

And invite whomever you met:
The lame, the maimed, the blind,
The cute. When so-and-so

Didn't show, you couldn't dis-
Invite the nameless multitude,
No more than death in a wink

Can blink away a life
Lived wide-eyed, each fantastic
Minute. The party must go on.

Wherever you were, it was loaves
And fishes. Lavish Kashmir
In frugal Massachusetts.

To you I was a woman
With an Irish past, who could talk
About those doughty nuns

From Mayo and Roscommon,
Charged with the scared duty
Of starving the budding hedonist

In you on the thin gruel
Of an ascetic Heaven, visions
Of gulls shrieking in Celtic Hell.

Over Assam and Earl Grey
I'd be held in the imperial sway
Of your captivating spirit,

Dispensing even mild
Criticism with a twist of wit
Or creamy smile and sugar.

"Darling," I can almost hear
You say, "Unlike your body
Your tea, or 'tay,' as the Irish

Charmingly put it, simply
Isn't hot enough. Let
Shahid help you out."

Sure enough, the next time
You came back (You always
Did return) from what

For simplicity you called home,
You brought for me alone
A sinfully plush tea cosy.

This winter has been bitter;
But my tea is hot, and it warms
My cup daily as I spirit

Myself back or forward,
As the case may be, looking
Hard at that present you gave me,

The complexity of crewel
Work, each twist the winding
Path on which you're climbing

Up and up through deep,
Satiating color—peacock, pine,
The ruby lips of that consummate

Couplet on the tip of your tongue,
As you approach the blazing
Snowfield near the summit.

American Shad

i.m. Julie Pratt Shattuck

We believe in patterns and need to believe it will happen
Again, so we fix the process with the word "spring".

No matter that the sweet and sour sounding May apple
Shatters April by baring a bone-white knuckle.

A burning bush, forsythia, predicts the miracle of food,
The current braving, dressed for battle, fasting American shad.

I had a friend who, when she remarried in her seventies,
Planted with her husband the wedding gift of a shad tree.

They've both since left, but the annual spawn of ghost petals
Still occurs when the magnolia lights its votive candles.

Yes, we believe the flower belongs to the stem, the stem
To the roots, that all things living and dead bear a name.

Carnevale

I had thought lots and lots
Of weddings must take place here,
Confetti in the sweet gelato
Colors of the villas on the hills,
Everywhere I walk trying to avoid
Myself along the *passeggiata di mare*.

Then a friend who knows more dropped,
"You sentimental fool. It's *carnevale* in Italy."
Ah, yes. Now I understand. One last
Fling. The assigned time to throw
Like variegated, dry snow
Caution to the wind.

You may not know it, though
I'll bet you do, but I've come to Italy
To prepare my soul to marry
You and have begun by marrying
Each day. (Church bells toll at all hours
I never knew were holy.)

I'm keeping a diary
Of events as they unfold
(A host of porpoises the other day)
Along this coast, where mountains plummet
Into ocean, dive into the hidden
Canyons of a vow.

Last Sunday I knew a man
In the village was raising the host,
Intoning "This is my body" and all I could do
Was think of you and that old couple
I saw drinking the sunset until
Every carnal drop was drunk.

Betrothal

It's a rare, still night
when a flame burns straight up,
no wavering. The date is set

for August. It's now late June.
Deep in the shaded heart
of the forest, laurel is blushing.

In the field out back, a sapling
shoots for the stars, while we
take supper under an old,

reposeful maple, millions
of fanning minions treating us
like royals on this close night.

Beads of sweat, seed pearls,
decorate a white wine glass,
glint in the light of our candle.

There'll be no veil, just naked
vows, a few good friends
instead of rows of melting candles.

This all came to me
as absent mindedly as morning
stroking your cool skin.

Absolution

The part of her that left is in the clouds,
Wild horses stampeding across the moon tonight
Headlong for the rim, manes and tails streaming
In a wind that shows how muscular the air can be.

The part that stayed is in this bouquet she created
Decades ago, hardly fading or fraying
Lilacs in pink and blue, the usual purple,
Saying I'll be this or that, I'll live forever,

Like the fused flower garland of the spine,
Running down the centre of a stripped pine table.
My husband sits on one side, me the other.
Even in silence our two plates touch her runner.

My forbearing grandmother still reining me in,
Though I'm forever leaping up to fling salt
On my latest sin against a cultivated moderation,
A red wine rose defiling her linen garden.

Even if I could unpick it thread by thread,
Lay her patience out like a corpse, she would remain
The knot of each uncomprehended day. My grandmother
Followed a pattern, walked in the way of her Lord

Stitch by stitch, the way she read with her finger
Under the words, though she could recite the Bible
As fluently as He had made creation in a week,
Not night after night, star after pinprick star.

Anniversary Campfire

High on a bluff over Lake Champlain,
dropped into a night so thick, the turncoat
air and viscous water lap as one,

I need my taciturn, steady woodsman,
a tree that's seen it all and stored it
in his core, whose leaves appreciate a breeze,

but knows how dangerous the wind can be.
He laid this pyre by light of day.
No sense foraging and fumbling in pitch

when one quick match, like a long
kiss after bitterness, can set the tinder
blazing, send heat scarabing on skin.

I'm trying to let go, to let the fire
consume the kindling of my nerve ends,
hearing, glimpsing, sniffing danger.

I'm leaning back in an Adirondack chair
named for the mountain range shape-changing
into bears and boulders over black water,

but the more I relax in this trickster
chair the more I leave my back
exposed to musket, bayonet and tomahawk,

Jeffrey Amherst's bateaux men rowing
from Crown Point, disease dripping
from their quiet oars, Montcalm in a fit.

Ambushed by panic, in a skirmish with myself,
I hear each twig snap, boot crunch, human
owl hoot, pittypat of moccasin and paw,

the prophet Tenskwatawa bursting through
the brush warning us to lay our long
knives aside forever or perish.

I have to speak. I can't take it
anymore, faking pleasure, "Honey,
could we go in? This isn't fun anymore".

"I'm scared too. I hate the dark,"
he whispers, his voice like a deer's nose
twitching, "but what scares me more

is that one stray spark might send the forest
up" (like one heated word,
I think, with us so over-wrought).

We stay. I concentrate on the eastern
discipline of being still while dying
of the fear, standing straight up in the flame.

We watch that fire take its course
from forked abandonment to embers,
all but the one stalwart log,

a bar of bullion eaten, a skeleton
of ash around a gleaming, holding on
beyond reason, fighting to rest in peace.

Derg

i.m. Kate Slattery

She took me to the edge, the middle
Of that God forsaken bog.
Together we would look out over

Unrepentant scree. Jesus
In his bare feet would have wept
To walk across it to the island.

I knew how it worked: ten
Hail Marys, an Our Father, plus
A Credo. Presto. You're walking on water.

In time, she'd go there on her own
And send me back kitsch souvenirs:
Her punishing excursion just a lark.

As though the matter in the air there,
Vulture hovering, were this
Or that, a simple either-or,

Her black and white post card read,
"Care package from a Pilgrim," then
"Enjoy," that forced pleasure my penance.

Now she's gone ahead of me
Again, this time to the last, dim
Island in the archipelago of stars.

Still, she sends me signals back,
A rock skipping across the surface
Of my peccant days and choppy nights.

Her wicked mimicry keeps hitting
The mark, then perpendicular
It drops, a bird in full flight shot,

Her voice years later in the restaurant
Sinking into crimson candor,
"The thing about cancer is it's interesting."

Floating

Two dragonflies, each floating
On a surf board willow leaf,

Nose to nose, those lovers
On inflated vinyl rafts,

Duellists at dawn, husband
And wife reunited at dusk.

Both can fly but don't.
This is the deepest part

Of the pond, the furthest point
From land. I'd best return.

Frog Spotting

for Meg, Hannah, and Grace Murphy

As a ghost appears to stir the air,
The atmosphere made rarer, they appear,

Mud creatures bubbling in the muck,
A tannic stew of dead and quick.

Hard enough with cave-dwelling eyes
To spot the first star at twilight,

Let alone a troll under the bridge.
But it's sunny now and I am with

My granddaughters by the beaver pond.
Education, fun, the pedagogue's compunction

To teach the young for as long as one can
The things one thinks they ought to learn.

Like how to spot a frog. Eyes roll
As I dive into the day's lesson, not at all

Hidden: camouflage and its corollary,
The need for the eye to be predatory.

"Shhhh," I caution as my raucous gaggle
In vivid, slapping flip-flops waddles

Near the sedgy edge, so close
The goo almost oozes between their toes,

A good thing too. You have to slip through
A vestigial gill slit, plop into

A foreign element, for it to leap
Out at you, a dead thing breathing.

So, my dears, swim in the obscure,
Eyeball to eyeball decide whether

Those bulging orbs mean sight or duckweed
Froth. Alight on every lily pad.

Let it happen. Spawn vision. Verdigris
Weathered copper secreted in green

Grass, a dun fuselage in sludge,
Periscope eyes, panoramic knowledge.

Above all remember it saw you
Before you saw it. So, before we have to

Part, for my sake please, try to see
Something where nothing appears to be.

Genoa

Our outermost layers fished from innermost
Drawers, closets, pockets emptied of us,

Then washed, scrubbed, rung, hung out
To dry, sin shriven and strung from high

Window to window in alleyways so tenebrous
And steep the sun may never reach them.

I'd say bunting but this is not a holiday.
It's everyday and everywhere that isn't home,

The lingua franca of clean laundry on a line
Making the most foreign of places home-like,

Old sheets not meant for company, dingy
Underwear not planned to meet an accident,

The flap of clothes unweighed by flesh,
Rising in the slightest breeze like Lazarus.

Telling the Time

A chrome sun, a snowfield,
An interrogation room,
Too much illumination
Bleaches things of scale.

Tussocks draped in sheets
Are alps, small drifts are dunes.
At four o'clock each plant,
Animal, and rock is doomed.

Mummified, khaki stems
Stand up knee deep in cloud,
The risen dead reporting
To the pearly gates.

All cast their black ink shadow
(Same ruler different
Nibs), each shaft inclining
In the one direction.

And the lines lengthen—see them—
As the town clock ticks,
Its face the lunar disc
A baby tracks for dear life.

Some believe that light
One day will see right through them.
Believe it or not, we all
Sign on the dotted line.

Why, you could tell the time
Right now by me, more or less
Accurately, a human gnomon
On a marble sundial.

Goldenrod

Come hither swaying. Salome. Someone's life
depending on resisting husky whispering
behind closed doors, a huge, unknown body
of water, whose breath you smell for miles through trees,
then flashing (dagger feathers? lucre?) in
and out of leaves, that word or phrase you cannot
for your life recall, that secret held
too well, too long, in the clenched fist of your tiny
existence, all your vaulted bullion in
the crack it takes an accident to happen blown
to the highest heaven, coming back, it all
comes back, as angel wings, celestial yellow
behind mundane green: an ocean of goldenrod.

My cup runneth over and over that moment
when I didn't stop, get off my bike,
walk out onto saffron clouds, sink
into a deep sleep in the ardent heat only
dying August generates the question why
give up a habit that's become as second
nature as breathing, thinking did I really
see it? Was it really there? Can anything be
so replete? Does every hedge conceal
an Elysian field? So I went on. My pedals
going round and round a problem that had been
a golden opportunity back there and then,
as fast and far away as I had come.

Anyway, why should I in a trice
rewrite every balking negative of history?
I didn't stop in the past for the arresting
lacquer shell of a box turtle saved
by my unthinking swerve, or the lone
buck of autumn seeping back into the dusk,
or the primordial beseeching of preverbal
peepers always heard and never seen, let alone
understood. No, I didn't step into that latest
breach, permit crazed dancers with feathers
on their heads nodding towards a truth
I know without the murder to bestow
their Midas touch on me, make me too happy.

Mourning Dove

A late May morning, the air fine muslin
already. So hot and humid each sound
travels with the underwater clarity of dreams.

Even the muted alto flute of my mourning
dove, velvet smoke rings, opium diffusing
sadness, carries like a goblet rung. Light taps

On the eardrum—"coo-coo-coo-coo-coo"
an anapest and spondee—"I see you, you,
you," the same line over and over again

like someone senile. What if we were no longer
able to recall the order—one, two, three,
four, five—or got cut off in midstream

from anticipation and fulfilment both (such perfect
love), would we also forget we have to
die? Your omniscience made me glass.

You told me not to tell a lie, then added
on a warning note, "Don't even think
about it. I can see right through you."

So, when I came to the home (prodigal, so long
away) to see you, I wasn't going to try
to explain my reasons: sickness, work. My life

didn't matter. All I feared and needed was to hear
my name; but your blue-veined lids, so like
a nursing mother's breasts, were deaf to me,

though you saw me in your way, like a blind
person who presents a test, such urges to do
evil: cock the snook, give the finger. I

could get away with murder. So why
the shame at my relief to see you dead
to the world? You wouldn't remember. I didn't

wake you. I walked back to the car, sealed
the windows up, began to sweat, leak, break
into tears—dry, staccato, jagged sobs.

A Heartbeat Away

My mother had a twin sister, brother, shooting star
Who died at birth, then took their mother to that place.
My mother lived looking in and running from a mirror.

I was the China doll with cherry lips that one day
Cracked into a lupine howl, sending my scared mother
Haring back into the black heart of the Black Forest.

Like wind or light she stalked me everywhere I went,
A certain leering behind trees, crazy cackling in the under
Brush, gnashing and weeping of branches and leaves.

Then I had a girl who hand-in-hand went out with me
Godless Sundays searching for shelter, a love maintained
At blood temperature. Even mothers can suffer from the cold

A stone's throw from home. A pine grove in a park
Sheering to the Irish Sea. Dried pine needles for a bed,
A natural pain like childbirth, softening over time.

"O sister dear, never fear," I'd say in our over-rehearsed,
Stilted, antique way. She'd reply, "O brother mine,
You are so brave and kind God will surely save us".

On and on pretending to wander without a clue
Through a green, free demesne on the outskirts of Dublin:
Purr of cars, screech of tires, sparrow chirp of other,

Obedient children skipping by their parents' sides,
The polite, sharp bark of diminutive dogs on tight
Leashes. Yet hard by the park decent people still expire

On high, mahogany beds in brick houses with gingerbread
Trim. Their agony observed by dry eyed, grim relatives,
A fire in the grate, the heavy, damask curtains drawn.

How on earth do we get back? Is my mother my father,
My sister my daughter, a girl a boy who sticks
A bony finger out between the bars to fox the mother

Who consumes her young, fattens babies for the kill?
We're all wicked stepmothers once in a while—a day,
A week, a month. Plus, show me the father who isn't weak?

And evil can taste very sweet. Yet most mothers relent
In the end, grant Gretel the starring part: shove
The old bitch into the oven, hear her foul flesh hiss.

The sky clears. A gray slate. The path out is obvious
And straight. "The witch is dead. The witch is dead," we whoop
And shout. God forbid my daughter say it of me.

A Little Lower than the Angels

At lunch we saw a hawk riding the thermals.
It was all I could do to go back, keep my vigil,

Watch my shrunken sparrow mother lug up
Winched buckets from her flooded lungs.

From our perspective, perched on a deck stuck
Like sticks into a mountainside, the hawk looked

Free of the godless gravity that keeps us fast
As magnets to this slope; but I was lost

To myself, back in her Baptist past, reading
The psalms to her at random, while I listened

In the slipstream of my own lost faith,
If not the words, which walk the earth, their wings,

The contours of the air known at discerning
Pinion tips. This is not a time to cavil,

But dominion over all the works of thy hand?
The mute shadow of that bird God's cursor?

Then it banks, rolls into the light, burns
Its name, brands its royal, crimson mantle

On our subject, upturned eyes, spirals, pivots
On an unseen string, lets the spirit move it.

Japonica

"…another little oddity is 'japonica'. The word, of course, merely means Japanese and we have a long and varied list of plants called so and so japonica. Popular taste, however, has attached the name specifically to the Japanese Quince.
C.E. Lucas Phillips

Like the rogue hair that keeps brushing my cheek
The way I used to try to coax you to suck,
I reach for a cause and my fingers comb the air,

The years, your thick, cascading, chestnut mane,
Sunlight playing in it like wrens in the undergrowth,
As you sit on my lap at breakfast in your uniform,
Cringing even before I raise the brush
To smooth the knot I knot tighter, cut
To the quick to be thought the agent of hurt, I inflict
A sharp, "We have to do something about this mop".

Like that unkempt bush flush beside the door
Snagging, scratching, tickling, going largely
Unfelt both in and out. As we can fail
To conceive of the person we conceived, I failed
To know its name until the "for sale" sign was down,
And it was too late for language to make a difference.

All that is but a snip away from this Christmas.
A brown river floods down your daughter's back.
You are the source and I'm an underground rumour.

Looking east over the Irish Sea on Stephen's Day,
Praying for a miracle, I spot at my feet that bush
Hacked radically back, shivering like me

When I see your white flesh exposed in winter
And there's nothing now a mother can say.

Back then I'd have to steel myself to enter
The jungle of your room when you weren't there.
God alone knew what monster might leap out,
The jaws of proof, fanged evidence of failure,
A mother afraid of the dark her daughter lived in.

I'd run back to the sunny, gravel paths of print,
Always intending to learn to garden: "The purposes
Of pruning are to maintain, increase or prolong
The vitality of the plant, or keep it in bounds, or direct
Its energy". But how to make a clean cut
With all these laterals of if, and, but, and or between
The new wood to be encouraged and the dead?

As the stars continue to shine despite our errors,
So, year after year those blossoms made it back,
Twinkling that pink in a galactic skein of branches,
A raw colour like a newborn's milk-chapped lips,
Or an insecure mother's cracked, useless nipples,
Still producing in that tangle sour, useful fruit.

I did find something truly terrifying in your room,
A lust for leafiness so rank it consumed
The cover of a dog-eared notebook, one boy's name
In a host of ivy scripts, innocence unchecked.

I might say now plain quince and be done with it,
But this blade of distance you've seen fit to insert
Between us has reduced me to a lovesick schoolgirl
Saying over and over, "Japonica, Japonica, Japonica."

High Tea

R.B.D. (Robert Butler Digby) Ffrench
(two fs, the first one upper case and silent)
once advised a student in the throes of psychosis
what he needed was a good, strong cup of tea.

Bob Ffrench also had the surpassing sense
to be late for his own funeral, the careening hearse
nearly killing the mourners driving back
from Kilternan, the bishop having blessed a void.

R.B.D. was probably enjoying a last cup of tea,
the better to serve with grace his time underground.
Hadn't another Butler, the Theosophist, denounced
"too much business with the passing hour" as swinish?

The remedy for ennui is tea, upper and downer
in one, the Age of Reason steeped, not
the turbo charge of coffee. Tea makes one less
logy than whiskey, vocal than the talking cure,

risk prone than champagne, more sanguine than wine,
alert than milk, satisfied than water. Gentle
and legal. High tea on high days and holy days
makes a body high as a body ought to be,

especially for one as Low Church as R.B.D.
Give him a thin sandwich between stained teeth,
not the priest with his host, ritual like a warm bath,
not the grave, conversation not rote liturgy.

R.B.D. would have died on the day to hear the Trinity
wit beside me quip, as the penny dropped
that something vital was missing, " I say, I've heard
of French without tears but never tears without Ffrench."

I thought I would die. I really did this year
round about the barren winter solstice, buried
alive by the mounting dark. I needed to resurrect
R.B.D. and his sister Nell, one of her piled high,

turf fire teas, invite company. I laid it out,
a corpse at a country wake on the dining room table,
the tastes I associate with nineteen sixty-nine,
my madeleines. My friends would be transported in spirit

if not the flesh. (Or is it the reverse?)
It would happen as we talk about the ins
and outs of marriage, kids. A bite, a sup
suffices for the whole, three-course performance.

They would get it as they get me, albeit
within my present boundaries. But this *mise
en scene* within the Pale, would it perhaps be
beyond it for them, even me still longing

for that place where all I seemed to do was long
for where I never did, never could belong:
a drawing room, rain against the casement,
a fire in the grate. My memory was scholarly.

Cracked, black pepper on wild, smoked salmon,
two terrines, one pork, one lentil, angels
and devils on horseback, celery, Stilton, ginger-
bread, apple tart, Christmas cake, and truffles.

All placed like a washed body on a linen shroud,
my Belfast tablecloth with the crochet border—
tea pot, cup and saucer, sugar bowl, and pitcher—
rhyming over and over like unbroken days,

or words that skate around a starched, slick,
empty center, the house newly-weds
move into, where every room is painted white,
the blank canvas of their bright future.

An Easter Egg

Before it happened, I imagined it
As an electric light switched on
In a dim cellar. The illuminating thing
Was seeing I'd been seeing all along,

Absorbed her comfort through my pores,
Gobbled glee off the plates of her eyes,
Suffered hunger pangs before she cried,
Fed her milk from one breast, honey

From the other. Then, the dove
Descended, brushed her blind lips and
She saw, tickled by that wing,
Appeared to view her mother as

Another. The angel, however, left her
A very special gift to be undone
A little at a time: a complete set
Of the bright building blocks of language.

And the first bit she unwrapped,
Raw gustatory bliss, was "mama".
Out of a mist of gibberish I fancied
I saw myself come into focus.

But she had been articulate as sunlight
Is of grass from the first dawn,
The logos of each gleaming blade.
Bee deep in a rose she'd squirm nectar.

By then she had the stones to build
With ever mounting skill the walls
That keep our weaned freedom safe
From the meddling breast of the world.

Still later, when our unrelated words
Bounced off consanguineous walls,
We'd flee the house and take to the road,
The laid down, written text of tarmac.

But one day, as a mother can go
Abruptly dry, our car sputtered
To a stop in the desert. My mouth is still
Parched and choked, packed with sand.

If to say a word were to lay an egg,
I'd try to speak that vessel—hard,
Autonomous, and fragile—food to start
Again, a foetal speck on the sun.

Feathers, Rocks and Bones

I have a shelf where I display
The booty of my necessary walks
Through owl deranged forests, blank
Beaches littered with the ocean's
Souvenirs of storms, rainbow feathers
Plundered from the sky, rocks washed
By the mantra of the tides to a Zen high sheen,
Bones bleached by being too seen.

And they have stitched me up before—
Needle and thread, talk and drugs—
But I have come apart again
Seeing you leave me as you came
Into this world in a headlong rush,
A fireball ripping through my body.

Today, dusting the abrupt emptiness,
The sight of a robin's-egg-blue shell
Ripped up the middle into halves,
The snip of foetal feather still
Albumen glued, attached, where the chick
Left, undid me. You must hold on.

Numb

I JEWEL

The story goes that it was sudden,
But it wasn't. It was more
Desultory than that, flipping through
July, finding the fresh daffodils
Of May already pressed and dried.

Death tiptoes through the drifts of sleep
To bless us with a quiet exit.
It was the way we actually age:
Our skin dries up by leaf degrees.
Snowflake by snowflake hair turns white.

So the days grew shorter and
The shadows longer long before
September. When she finally found
The will to hold the creosoted mirror
Up, disaster was all but complete.

If she dares now to compare
This present desolation to
A tepid mishap long ago,
You may determine she deserves
Her frigid fate. But hear her out.

She'd lost an earring in a dim city
After dark. The next morning, she
Retraced her steps, then re-retraced them,
Searching for the smallest glimmer,
Loath to endure a loss forever.

So, with her daughter. They used to be
A pair, worse, the one, rose gold pendant.

II SEEDPOD

Demeter at the end of October.
She who spent so lavishly
Now spent, the luxury, to think,
Of just one rose, let alone the flor-
Abunda summer. Bankrupt, barren,

Broke. She has to start today
To reconstruct a life, save,
Steward her resources, thrifty
Seedpods, skinflint straw, be
As bleached and bloodless as the landscape.

Practice beige restraint. More,
Accomplish it with what's at hand.
Not caring what she fells or floods,
Be there for the child to come back to
As surely as the roses will return.

First, repair the breaches in
Her barriers, shore her tears, build
Not just one, several dams.
Use every last limb, log, and twig
In the confused forest all around her.

She'll come out at night, exit
Underwater, look like the bark she eats,
Snout iron in the silver moonlight,
Work, work, work in sleep until
The dawn of what they call the day

Then sleepwalk static in her lodge,
Mud and wood, skin and bone: home.
She'll stay with it the way she stayed
One whole winter between white
Sheets in a grey, drizzly city

Waiting for the snow child to be born.
Demeter kept her legs together
Tight as a burning, ivory novice,
All to concentrate, to gestate
The full-term rose explosion.

III ZEN NOVEMBER

Blood soaked rags on the horizon,
The blue heron and her mirrored
Double posing for eternity.

November. A daughter ripe as August
Gone. Her distraught mother turned
The world to stone to be less lonely.

The beaver pond beyond twilight.
Basalt mountains, agate water,
Bone tree trunks, limestone moon.

Her own making, but it's hard,
The interval before grief speaks,
The first, frozen teardrops fall.

But harder still when it begins
To crack, detonations, gravel
Pocks, overlapping ripples, chaos.

Only this is from below, far down,
Deep, as far as you can go,
Where the primal magma boils and bubbles.

Muscled arcs of black starvation,
Leaping up involuntary as a sigh,
Punctuating minnow commas,

Giving pause, a certain obscure
Pleasure, the taste of your own blood,
The sight of skin, that vast, elastic surface.

IV BREACH

As thin as foetal finger
Nails, the first December
Ice, blistered, taut,
The skin of a burn victim.

The sun didn't torch
This surface used to feeling
Every little gust
And nibble, wave and ripple

Senseless. This was from
The pit, infernal heat,
So off the charts it circled
Back and stunned water.

Our softer nature searching
In a cracked mirror sees
Each human kindness twisted,
Hardened, and reversed.

Hot is cold, summer
Winter, light dark,
Brother blind to brother,
Mother and daughter dead

To each other. The mother lives
On what she now considers
Viable terrain, life
May be said to prosper where

An order is maintained.
A Spartan stubble field,
Tree limbs stripped and scoured,
The laundered light of winter.

The daughter lives beneath
The spell of that inimitable
Voice, furry haunches,
Angel face, the mother wants

Only to forget
But can't no more than vacate
That blood brocaded chamber
She and her daughter still share.

V   SICK JANUARY

It's not the way she planned it.
A thick tarpaulin of ice
Stretched from shore to shore,
Hermetic as an eardrum.

A full moon on glass, ghostly
Light haloing the flayed
Bodies of the damned,
An overall, opal gloaming.

But most of all a vitreous
Surface to walk across
And see finally what might be
On the other side,

Or in a fit of self-
Possession skate, indite
Deep-cut, cryptic arabesques
On pure white paper.

But this ice doesn't take
Like grief that won't solidify
As January rage, then melt
As tender April's tears.

It's watery, anaemic, weak.
No sooner does it stiffen
Its resolve then shrink back
Bullied to a thin puddle

By that clamor down below,
The unholy, faux summer,
Hammer beat, the over-
Heated rhetoric of Lucifer.

She needs it to be so cold
The hyper-active fish slow down,
And over-protected turtles
Womb down deeper into muck.

Demeter without her daughter
Is with her daughter in hell.

VI THE KILL

The tai chi of the heron,
As she ballet trawls
Crepuscular for supper.

The soundless breeze of lifting
One, Angle-poise, lead
Leg after another.

Knife insertion, blade clean
Strokes, slow motion rowing
Over a pond of patience.

Everything is preparation,
Learning to endure
The atmosphere of living

Underwater. Feather
Breaths that stick like rocks
In a constricted throat,

Interminable neck,
The length of time despair
Can take before it fish flashes

Look, here, hunger,
Something smaller but better
Than wishing you were dead.

VII BAG OF CATS

Demeter is on her knees praying
For the ground to freeze well below
The frost line, down to its very core,
No longer porous, stone deaf, numb
To the child's kitten whimpers on
The other side with him, the fiend,
Old enough to be her father.

When summer was forever, Demeter
Never cleaned the house or got
The cats spayed. Then the child's
Favorite, a mother surrogate, had
Her litter in a loose sling of hop
Sacking bellying under the marriage
Bed. The slit-eyed, fur-fused clutch

Importuned Demeter, spoiled her selfish,
Suckling sleep. Inadequate even
To a bag of cats they'd drown down
The country. She put the lot in a basket
By the fire, then one by one by the scruff
Of the neck their mother brought them back,
Safe in the place where they'd been born.

VIII GERIATRIC TRANSPORT

She doesn't have to fly,
Just twist her neck to look
Like Lazarus, dead wood alive.

And, when it's hot, an old guy
In Bermuda shorts, spindly
Shanks, pot belly, beak.

Androgynous with age
She's sexless Queen Victoria
With wide piazza wings

Which, open, are an ostrich
Fan, a tasselled shawl
In indigo that grows

Bluer with a loss
Of light, slate presuming
It can rise above

It all, unfurl its serpent
Neck into a vector
And then shoot for the sun.

Instead, one night, when twilight
Weighs like smoke, she has
A go, begins to flap

Laboriously trying
To shift that burden from
Her bosom's granite ledge,

Defy their expectations,
Show them the old bird
Still knows how to fly.

IX PREMATURE

They've been tricked.
Unnatural.
So warm they're back
Before it's safe.

The bald infant
Heads of bulbs
Crowning prematurely,
Tumescent buds,

Eager flowers
Under still sad
Trees. It's usual
For ice to come

To this, to crack
Wide open
Before brown
Gives way to green,

But they should wait
Until this erratic
Season passes,
Until things

Are petal frilly
Enough for a baby
Daughter. She
Could get a blast,

A neurotic fit
Of frost, a freakish
Fall of snow
Could bury her

Alive. The readiness
Was never mine
Queenly to
Decree. My time

Came like weather,
The blank, new born
Stare of March,
The scorching brow of August.

Honesty

I don't believe I've seen it
This early in the season.
Not unequivocal monocles.
Rather, tarnished pennies,
Petty lies, mounting up
To penury. Not so fast.
Opaque of me not
To see we too may grow
Into transparency.

Lent

Ash Wednesday in Camogli.
A fisherman sits on a stone wall
In the harbor mending a net.

He holds like a China cup
In his man-sized, callused hands
A shuttle wound with thread.

I assume it's strong. It's also
Thin, strength deriving from the cell
Principle of a beehive, geometric

Dawn to noon to dusk to midnight
Days that hold the otherwise
Intolerable weight of a life.

His sea eyes search far
Beyond the rainbow-painted, hope
Anchored, wildly tossing boats.

His land eyes mind the work
To hand—ghosts are punishing
This coast, rising up, evaporating

Rocks. A time to mend,
Weave in and out like waves,
Or the swaying net underwater,

Quite invisible. How does he know
Where it's been rent? So intricate
And fine and folded over time

And time again like a man
Tanned and whipped and ground
To sand by sun, salt and wind.

Repairing is his way of making
And remaking the same, seamless,
Original net he can barely

Remember or know for sure—
Will the catch hold? One fat,
Pre-lapsarian fish slip through?

Malamute

Weather sent to temper us.
Tonight the door to the North
is ajar and the polar blowtorch
blasting through a crack.

It's now we know zero
is more than a barren concept,
not nothing when there can be
less than this perfect nothingness,

minus our hand-to-mouth,
hacking cough of an existence,
strung between one thermometer
and another, mercury and blood.

And in between this small
benefit: the malamute out back,
who always seems nostalgic
for the Arctic, is right at home,

lifting his splintered howls
to the human looking moon,
emitting ice-pick yaps,
chipping away at what's inside him.

Painting Blind

Those who used the vessel knew the story
And believed in the scheme that made sense of it.
The son of a god, the God of gods, slain.
What better explanation than the father
Let it happen? A long war costs, should cost
Everyone. A wise deity will suffer loss,
Bow to fate. So Zeus threw his son to the dogs.

Blood gushes from the young man's spear tip wounds
In straight, fine, narrowly spaced, radiating
Lines, grace from a martyr's breast, the sun
Blessing all of us regardless. Sarpedon
Has fallen, flesh fired to a terracotta leaf.
Avarice has stripped him of his armor, made him
Ready to fall further softly or to fly.

Sleep and Death are on either side sporting
Beaked eagle helmets, heron wings,
Ideal gear for high altitude air
Transport. While subtle Hermes in his cock-spur,
Bee-wing sandals makes it possible to walk
On water, hover inches from the earth,
Skim it like a hand over warm skin.

A human being painted this. It is he
Who made in quick strokes like the tick of a clock
The calyx of this fragrant body, sniffed
With the tip of a hummingbird swift instrument
The sloe ripe testicles, sable pubic nest,
Pectorals like the turtle's back, sinew strung
Sweet sounding box, ambrosia we can smell,

Sweat we taste, a visual banquet painted
Blind, by this I mean how each of us
Must live, midnight pressing on our burning
Daylight, the air pressure that keeps us together,
The clear solution Euphronius had to draw with
Disappearing into wet clay like rain into dry
Earth, like one drop of blood in the ocean.

All would be revealed when it had passed
Through fire in three efficient stages. One,
Let air into the kiln. The worst did not
Happen. The object blushes clay. Two,
Burn green wood, cut off the air. Smoke
Chars the lot. It did occur. Three, let air
Back in and a sublime balance is restored:

Flesh as blood against black circumstance.
The artist couldn't see all this beforehand.
He guessed where he had been and should go next.
Like Troy and Greece, blind hope and eagle-eyed
Experience, the ghost lines merge at last;
But the greater of these by far is hope. So he
Is blessed who fails to see yet still believes.

Ups and Downs

for Harriet O'Donovan Sheehy

For a short while I lived
in a land of longevity.
The people there ate nothing
but the greenest greens
drizzled with liquid light,
plucked perpetually ripe
fruit at arm's length
from wide open windows,
slaughtered just enough
animals to satisfy the dark
places in the soul, rolled
their dough communion wafer
thin, then cut it into
fanciful shells and spirals.
But I'll remember it
the most for how the old
taught me by example
how to manage all those
steps, no two alike,
this minute and the next,
wide, narrow, shallow,
steep, uneven, level,
dry and wet from unseen
weeping, blind corridors
Brailled by moss zig-
zagging to an unseen end.
I knew there must exist
for each up near the ridge,
where frayed treetops feather

into sky like worry
into sleep a box
wrapped in the soft pastel
of coffin silk and tied
with a scentless flower frieze,
the gift of home, the place
where we repair ourselves,
then start, no sooner rested,
to prepare for yet another
foray down and up,
a peril in both directions.
Slip and it can be
suicide. Back is a heart
attack waiting to happen.
Still, we take the risk
again and again until
the manifest conclusion.
It would be so easy
to sink into the duck down
sea at our feet than keep
on climbing. The grass
grows sparser, turns
to rock, then thins to air.
Still we carry on,
up and up, one step
at a time. We stop
at each, take in the view,
the sharp slope of memory,
another day alive,
resist the tic of looking
up, measuring what's left.
No, head down, dogged,
we persist, the next,
the one after that, two

bulging, plastic, pulmonary
sacs for balance and
for company the reassuring
beat, the idle chat,
or desperate thud, of that
familiar (sometimes quite
irregular) stranger in
our breast, our only friend
on such necessary journeys.

Cardinal Sin

A sudden gash
Of lipstick slashed
Across the bedroom
Mirror, failing
Once again
To see the other,
Wiser me,
Brown cowering
In a bush.
I am known
For attacking
My own reflection.
I forget
Myself sometimes.

Red Feather

Like the stained tip of a bayonet
she sports it on her hat,
brandishing her plunder at the sky.

Or is that blood actually
gushing from her head
a sign of haemorrhaging within?

Has a bloodbath boiled up
outside the picture's frame
spattering the grass with columbine?

The artist makes us desperate
to invade a woman painted
impregnable as daylight.

Buttercups and daisies, dead
faces on a battlefield, look up
to observe our lady, as she passes

among them, descending a steep
incline, lit from behind,
each frail stem incarnadine.

Is the sun rising or setting?
Are we looking east or west?
Are we on the coast or inland?

We can be forgiven
for thinking we feel the salt tang
of a sea breeze on her cheek,

for it is written Winslow Homer
painted Maine, but what
can print or paint really tell us

of a lady, that her arched eyebrows,
held down by her brim, join
in the pale beyond as wings?

That her pink mouth, wound
and cupid's bow, darts deadly
kisses and attracts them back?

No, hatted, snooded, skirted,
cloaked, presumably gloved and booted,
she is under wraps,

bares nothing but her naked,
generically pretty face,
veiled by an air of introspection.

Is she mother, sister, lover,
daughter, wife or forever
patient, chaste betrothed?

Even her carnal arms,
tucked in the tent of her thought,
are no more than outline.

Just the slight beginning
or the ending of a smile
betrays her, a leaf considering

or reconsidering unfurling.
That stabbing in the ocean of her petticoat,
that swaying in the seaweed of forsythia,

that gold braid, abrupt
flash of dashing scarlet
have, for the most part, left her

wed to protective plumage,
menstrual crimson and maroon.
Her hands rest on her stomach.

She walks to the swing of a pendulum.
Soon she must go home,
go in, escape our view,

close the hall door behind her,
slip the weapon of her hatpin
from its nest, observe the globe

of a woman in the dusky glass
turning to ask the cardinal
question, "Who is that lady?"

A Drop of Water

Margaretta Haverman,
I didn't come here to find you,
As close to an unknown as water
Is to air, I came for greatness:
Whirlpool stars, ecstatic grass.

But I'm married as a Dutch
Matron to a man who sees
Paint on canvas as a fact,
An insect or a leaf, to be
Inspected with a rapt attention.

So, we started out in Italy,
The gold and azure fifteenth century,
And slowly as a rock erodes
Have made it up to the Low Countries
In the black and white eighteenth.

A girl threads her soul through a needle.
The great world yellows on a wall.
A maid looks toward a blushing window.
The framed picture in the picture
Frame might be the Last Judgment.

Interiors bring out the arsonist in me.
But flower paintings make me happy,
That ladylike sub-genre tucked
Into the still life corner of a numbered
Room, a grave in Potter's field.

Once upon a time, a woman
In a long, white nightgown wandered
Out at dawn into her garden
And gathered into her flat basket
All the life it could contain.

But somewhere between out and in
She sinned, according to my husband,
For whom mimesis is paying your taxes,
Not mortgaging the truth to tact.
It's there, he says, in the anachronism.

Don't be fooled by the striated
Tulip with exactly the right degree
Of streakiness in its claret stripe.
Tulips don't grow next door to cabbage
Roses. The whole thing's been contrived.

Don't be tempted by the misted
Grapes, the furry peach. Don't flinch
Before the beetles, bees and ants.
That wasp doesn't sting. That snail
Is trapped inside a shell of artifice.

I look. The shellac is so glassy
Thick I think I see myself
In it, my just-out-of-bed spiderwort-
Mullein-birds-foot-trefoil hair,
Margaretta Haverman

Looking wild as her countryman,
Who torched a cypress tree to watch it
Burn forever, never be consumed,
To turn the outside in and inside
Out, to make the sun dilate

72

Like the eye seeing it. So close,
I almost brush away a drop
Of water I think mars the art,
Then understand it's there to look like
Trust welling in an artless face.

Room 5, the Bonnard Show

All those years, encrustations, residue, thick layers
Of paint, rust flaking on an iron bedpost. To think

Of those emerald mules he'd have you slip into after
Your bath, the better to show you off in your buff,

Or black pumps, or purple slippers, ingenious levers
Giving you that boyish kilter, arch of back, tilt of rump.

Recall the old days on Rue Lepic in Paris,
The permanent chill of standing in that oval, zinc tub,

Venus on the half-shell for the world's consumption.
They are still trying to pry, to prize you free.

Audiocassettes, astute comments, but it's the artist
They've paid to see, the man behind the scintillate facade,

A human being whose idea of living was having adventures
Of the optic nerve, who had the nerve to relegate you

To the margins of the garden, sparrow brown, sunk
In thought, while she, Renée, the other woman, reigned

As sun goddess, ripe and blond, her ruddy cheeks
Rhyming with the juicy apples on the table within easy

Reach of him as well, invisible, but he's the reason
For her wistful smile and central position, why you exist

In profile, clipped by the frame; for you were in
His life and she long dead, "suicide," they said, "drowned

In her bath". You filed the image quietly away,
Married your Pierre, became the artist's wife: clay

To be fired and glazed. What better things had you to do
Than watch your own flesh petrify, become a statue

Under the touch, the merest brush, of his lustful eyes,
Fondling your rock-hard, half-moon breasts, their pebble

Nipples, smudged pubis, gleaming, marble mound
Of Venus, barest hint of an infernal slit. Injustice

After injustice, to be given that thick, unerotic
Waist and neither chick nor child to show for it,

That unseductive, helmet bob, static as plastic,
Pug nose, plug legs, the overall, plain shape

Of a clothespeg. Prior to you he'd ordered a model,
"Live in front of me. Forget that I exist."

There had to be a loss. There had to be a central
Void for there to be a picture, he'd instruct

And you'd oblige, became an empty conch shell
To yourself, high and dry, a roaring in your head.

These are true interiors. He said it was you;
Both of you, in fact, feared the vertiginous blur

Of the world, preferred the busy patterns, fuzzy maze,
Out-of-focus checks and stripes of your domestic life,

The camouflage of rugs, screens, throws, furniture,
Upholstery, draperies, tablecloths, wallpaper, paintings

And you to play an everyday Marsyas (note
The putrid, greenish undercoat) flayed by his eyes.

They stalked you everywhere, the more mundane the task
The better, drying off after your bath, setting the table,

Sewing, dressing. You'd be daydreaming; he'd whip off
Those wire-rim specs for five minutes of antic sex,

Then the great divide resumed. There is no place
Like home. Fifty-four years of this invasive distance.

Far easier to wrest reflection from the water's face
Than your hunger from that of your ravenous voyeur,

Hovering together over the abyss, the two wings
Of a madly flapping hummingbird manufacturing its bliss,

Chasing each other every which way across an empty
Canvas. "We only fixate," he would preach, "on moving

Targets." You'd be tempted to beseech him then to give
His restless retina a rest, desist from all these quick,

Saccadic movements, look you level in the eye just once,
Then just as quick dismiss the idea as suicide,

Equally fatal as a total lack of ocular connection.
One blink and you'd be on the brink of extinction.

He was right. The eye was binary, couldn't hold
In simultaneity the two ends of the spectrum, which is why,

He'd vow, as an artist, I will never let you
Die (or live, you had to reply under your breath).

This is a man who made a blue so bright it had to be
White in direct sunlight. How could he possibly see

That you'd been bleached to monomania by him,
That being clean again had become your obsession?

You took to your bath. He followed you and let us
In. This was the conclusion he had needed you all along

To imagine for him. Tiles glittering like a mermaid's scales,
An array of cold surfaces: linoleum, glass, enamel,

Plus the scalding, numbing, catafalque of water
Misting his lenses like true sorrow or a sign of life,

For she had never been more herself, sinking deeper
And deeper, floating higher and higher on sensate pain,

Front and center reclaimed. Her power makes the tub
Obey the contours of her minnow mute, svelte lozenge

Of a now diminished body. She is an old, old star
Radiating stored-up energy, magnetizing every eye.

First, she bled between her thighs, then between her words,
Now she is haemorrhaging her most fabulous colors yet

For him. Even the neutral grout between the tiles leaks
A coruscating teal, lime, gold, mauve, violet, electric

Blue. Splashes of scarlet on the floor and in the swirling
Water make it look like a slit wrist has gushed anger.

This is the most vibrant, violent palette he has ever
Used and all to prove that it is her not him, here

And here and here again, risen, wherever I turn
A woman like a brittle curse thrown against a wall

And shattered, the only tear she ever managed to shed
For herself, carved by him into its myriad, brilliant facets.

Red-Winged Blackbird

He cuts across my path,
Coming at me sideways,
Streaming for the swamp,
That bombed out city.

Motionless, he's poised,
A trigger cocked for life
Or death, a sentry high up
On his charred pinnacle.

Pinions tucked, he over-
Looks the scene—infantry
Of frog spawn, reconnaissance
Of dragon flies—and smoulders.

Nobody would guess.
His bloodless shoulder blades
Are boomerangs that circle
Back questioning his name.

So disciplined when he's
At ease only the sun
Can see his stygian iridescence,
Wanton other life.

Then, under sudden
Marching orders only he
Can hear he's off, wings
Flared, epaulets ablaze.

Each time the recognition fresh,
Reading what you know
But didn't know you knew.
I never see it coming:

Words that fly, words
That drop, nothing like
The wordless surge, the arc
Of lustrous, preening anger.

Schoolhouse Clock

I bought it when our friend fell gravely ill,
Tick-tock. Not just the time to know the hour
But hear each grain of sand remaining drop.

I brought it home, a baby from the hospital,
Tick-tock, wrapped in a blanket, its big head
And short torso housing its pendulum heart.

We hung it in the kitchen, my oak clock,
Tick-tock. I needed its open face, the march
Of its Roman numerals for this latest test.

It was every three-minute egg decisively swiped,
Tick-tock, the *Times*, bread toasted to a glow,
Hot tea, the precise way to start each day.

And after dark, the sweet, reliable man,
Tick-tock, who came to my door at dusk and stayed.
Now we both sit under that stern instructor.

I set it, wind it, give its brass a little nudge,
Tick-tock, and like a year-old ready to walk
The thing takes off and I no longer exist.

Worse, given any tension, it thunders its
Tick-tock, winds the unsaid up to such a pitch
The kitchen is a time-bomb set to go off,

Which is not to say there aren't still summer meadows,
Tick-tock, of eternal bliss. The long grass hours
Wave and I drift off into a buzzing trance,

Forgetting every chore, like winding that clock,
Tick-tock. It stops and I can't understand time
Daring to pass when there's a corpse in the house.

Garden Tour

Never to know the certain
refuge of a screened gazebo.
Never to cross an arch-
backed bridge into Kyoto.
That gate, cast iron bars,
bare branches of a winter
tree, was always locked,
that shade too thick to penetrate.

Maybe it was my scare
(the too bright lights
of an operating theatre)
but suddenly I was in it,
on the garden tour, with all
the other women my age,
and the slim, well-tended owner
in the wide-brimmed, canvas hat,
ever-ready, sharp secaturs
dangling, a pistol on her hip.
Leaving us free to wander.
There, if we needed her.

At first I couldn't see
beyond the sameness, greenness,
ice and snow, which, of course,
are quite distinct whites.
Then looking became more
like listening to another's talk.

I saw bleeding hearts,
their swaying fronds, a city
street, each flower heart-

breakingly sweet, all the same,
and a Japanese maple rusting
just by virtue of its species,
and skyscraper ferns leaning
gracefully into their fate.
and the speckled leaves of lungwort
breathing out as dappled moss.

Foliage began unfolding
one leaf at a time,
enfolding me into that cool,
umbrageous underworld,
a shade among shades.

"How do you cope?" I had to
ask. "I don't. I relish it.
My husband, before his sickness,
was a massive man.
Bare-handed he would shift
rocks, sink posts,
tote compost sacks.
No burden was too great.
My partner does his best,
but his heart isn't in it."

Still, I had to press her,
since shade is all, the little
that I have, to reveal
her most shrouded secret.

"To be honest, some people say
they play the hand they're dealt.
I disagree. I never plant
anything that won't give me
three seasons of pleasure."

It was then I saw
her hand brooding over the face
of her creation, the raw
flesh of a shag bark maple
next to holly blood
on snow, the tarnished copper
of a blue spruce spire.

"I have to take it back.
I always plan for winter.
We have so much of it here."

The Week Before Thanksgiving

for Susan and Glenn Johnson

Still savage, shunning touch.
Waking to the dawn interrogation.
Getting up to go downstairs to eat
breakfast on my own, tea and toast,
the news, the latest on the war,

I get no further than the bottom
step. Hit by black bee bees
in my sleep-wide, bleary eyes. Shot,
I limp behind my body, take
some time to form the words a pane
of glass away—"Wild turkeys."

"Come down," I holler up, needing him
to see this sign which we've been given,
more fitting for the likes of us
than Noah's dove and olive leaf.

Apparently, turkeys can be Love's emissaries
too, sent to bless the cursed
descendants of Sodom and Gomorrah.

This Tom, these hens, one, two, three four, five,
six, seven, eight, nine, ten, each
with a sideways bead on us, compose
a firing squad eliminating sin.

See how they parade, these sombre,
regimented creatures, who may know
the first may be the last one day
but today the order of the day
is order *per se*, no power plays.

But why, I ask, is the first first?
Not bravery necessarily. That would be
obvious. Maybe just the best nose?
And those lost in the middle? Surely not
the mediocre? Rather good communicators,
sure to pass the word from front to rear,
providing a clear line of command.
And the last but never least? Please not
the most reviled, the weakest. Perhaps just
she who is best at covering her ass.

And how do they maintain the discipline,
keep formation, stay married,
mere steps away from the little remaining
wilderness in town, when their dun undertaker
clothes give off the whiff of leaf
decay? Could it be they embody
order, down to their sabre tail feathers,

where arrowheads march sharper and sharper,
smaller and smaller up to the brink,
go over the top? That's how close
you have to come to see, if not
to touch, the spurt of scarlet wattle.

Why is it, I have to ask, we need
to see red to think restraint?

CPSIA information can be obtained at www.ICGtesting.com
Printed in the USA
LVOW060935090513

333005LV00001B/211/P